THEATRE CENTRE

B**THE**RDER

BY AFSANEH GRAY

First performed at
Redbridge Drama Centre
on 12 September 2019

The Border

Cast

Julia **Jazmine Wilkinson**

Mother, Mayor, Female Borderguard, Stranger **Rujenne Green**

Father, Refugee Boy, Journalist, Male Borderguard **Matt Littleson**

Grandma, Smuggler, Jogger, Call Centre Boss **Lucie Capel**

All other characters and social media interludes will be performed by the company ensemble.

Creative Team

Playwright **Afsaneh Gray**

Director **Natalie Wilson**

Designer **Alice Hallifax**

Composer **Ted Barnes**

Lighting Designer **Neill Brinkworth**

Movement Director **Ingrid Mackinnon**

Dramaturg **Sarah Dickenson**

Production Manager **Faith Austin**

Company Stage Manager **Robert Browning**

Theatre Centre Staff

Artistic Director and Joint-CEO **Natalie Wilson**

Executive Director and Joint-CEO **Raidene Carter**

Participation Producer **Joseph Raynor**

Programme and Administration Coordinator **Lucy Goodman**

Marketing Officer **Kat Rodda**

Director's Introduction

In 2018 we pushed out a provocation into the playwriting world in the form of the remodelled Brian Way Award. We invited writers to give us ideas on the theme of Treaty. Throughout that year, we were immersed in World War One and the Armistice commemorations as we toured *The Muddy Choir*, by Jesse Briton, across the country. Our thinking was that after Armistice comes Treaty and that this focus would offer us a rich progression in our commissioning. With 2019 gearing up to be a tumultuous year for possible new Treaties with our nearest neighbours, we wanted our new play to feel the pulse of the times we live in.

The response was fascinating, with the interpretation of Treaty ranging from the domestic to the dystopian. *The Border* by Afsaneh Gray stood out as a concept. The idea to take this impossibly complex theme and to distil it into a simple parable about a girl who loses her dog captured our imagination and attention. Meeting Afsaneh and interrogating the idea only made us more excited. The treatment not only gave scope for immense theatricality but also suggested a unique disruption mid-performance to kick off a conversation with the audience. Theatre Centre's ambition has always been to keep stretching ourselves, our audience and the form itself and *The Border* offers such a stretch.

Now we have the draft play, ready for rehearsal, *The Border* is clearly more than a simple parable. Afsaneh's writing challenges us to wake up to the system that puts value on "having stuff" at the expense of our humanity. This play digs deeper than a political decision to build a border. It invites us to search for new meaning in our society by listening and learning from things and people that may at first appear strange but with time and patience will become the new familiar. It calls on individuals to be better as people and not to rely on the systems and institutions that sell themselves to the highest bidder or flirt with whoever is prepared to pay the share price.

The Border is exuberant, absurd, ridiculous in places but holds a truth that needs to be spoken. Division is real, but we can find a way back; but only if we don't follow blindly those who don't have our best interests at heart. We need to question those in positions of power and make up our own minds about the big issues of our age. To be presenting the play to young audiences is an honour and we want the play to start a conversation that ultimately gives young people the agency to decide what kind of world they want to shape for today and tomorrow.

Playwright's Introduction

We are living in an extreme, and extremely confusing, world. Everything and everyone is at top volume. Events move at such a pace that it's like we're on fast forward. As an adult, I find this overwhelming. So, it's hard for me to imagine what it's like to be coming to maturity in this extraordinary din. I grew up in the 1990s, a time of studied apathy, when the centrists had won, and we were supposed to be post-political. That's not an option for young people today. The effects of decisions taken by politicians are all too relevant for their lives and their futures.

With *The Border*, I wanted to create a pause. A moment to sit back and consider the terrifying absurdity of this moment in history – when all we hear are meaningless soundbites and so everyone's stopped listening. How do we find meaning in what's deliberately meaningless? How do we truly listen to each other and find thoughtful responses in a world that's so thoughtless? How do we inform ourselves in a world full of disinformation? These are the challenges we face today. Somehow, I wanted to capture that in this play – and the simple story of a girl who loses her dog seemed like the right vehicle for that. Because as much as we would like to ignore the maelstrom outside the window, we all have to face up to it. It's affecting our families, our communities, our world. And if it isn't yet, then it soon will be. This is what Julia – the heroine of this play – discovers. And if she learns how to navigate the crazy world we have created with grace and kindness, then I think we can too.

Acknowledgements

I wrote *The Border* in the year after having my first child. If it hadn't been for the secure knowledge that I would be supported every step of the way by my wonderful partner, Gabriel, I would never even have attempted it. I am also indebted to my mother, Nicoline, Adam, Alexander and assorted siblings and niblings for always having open arms for my baby, leaving me free to write. Thanks to Natalie Wilson, Sarah Dickenson, and the whole Theatre Centre team, whose faith in me and in this play has been unwavering. Thanks to Ted Barnes, for his beautiful music. And finally, thanks to Giles Smart – I couldn't wish for a better agent.

I'd also like to thank all the actors involved in the development of the play: Aryana Aramkhalawon, Natasha Cowley, Ella Dunlop, Michael Lyle, Siobhan McSweeney and Elexi Walker, as well as all the year 12 students from the BRITschool and Year 9 students from Nicholas Chamberlaine School in Bedworth.

Jazmine Wilkinson | Julia

Jazmine trained at Rose Bruford.

Credits include: *Shakespeare in Love* (UK Tour), *Christmas at Kew* (Kew Gardens), *Gilgamesh* (The White Bear Theatre), *Shadow Games* (UK Tour), *Drafters* (Jazz Central, New York).

Theatre whilst training includes: *Lion in the Streets*, *The Crucible*, *Vinegar Tom*, *Strange Fruit* (Rose Bruford) and *The Caucasian Chalk Circle* (Syracuse University, New York).

Short films include: *Popped, The Train, The Veins in her Eyelids, Bad Friends, Like Brother, Like Sister, The Sermon*. Other notable credits include web series *The Art of Dating* and lead female in music video *Pray* by Tora Kamanja.

Rujenne Green | Mother, Mayor, Female Borderguard, Stranger

Rujenne studied at Mountview Academy of Theatre Arts.

Theatre credits include: *Square Rounds* (Finborough Theatre), *The Dog Beneath the Skin* (Jermyn Street Theatre), *Cookies* (Theatre Royal Haymarket) and *The Alchemist* (Neuss Globe Theatre).

Matt Littleson | Father, Refugee Boy, Journalist, Male Borderguard

Matt has recently graduated from Mountview.

Theatre whilst training includes: *Punk Rock, The Glass Menagerie, Measure for Measure* and *On the Shore of the Wide World*.

Lucie Capel | Grandma, Smuggler, Jogger, Call Centre Boss

Lucie studied at the Moscow Art Theatre School in 2017 and has just graduated from the ArtsEd MA Acting course.

Theatre whilst training includes: *The Cherry Orchard, Andorra* and *Antony and Cleopatra* (ArtsED). *The Border* is Lucie's first professional engagement.

Afsaneh Gray | Playwright

Afsaneh is a playwright and screenwriter. She is currently under commission by the Unicorn Theatre and the BBC. Her 2017 production *Octopus* transferred to London's prestigious Theatre503 after a hugely successful run at the Edinburgh Fringe Festival. Afsaneh was the recipient of Theatre Centre's 2018 Brian Way Award Commission and *The Border* is her first play for the company.

Natalie Wilson | Director

Natalie has been Artistic Director of Theatre Centre since 2007. She has led the company into a new era, refreshing the company's vision to make young people's activism a key driver of the artistic programme. Having overseen more than 20 new commissions at Theatre Centre, her work with playwrights has been largely steered by this mission and has been recognised by the Writers' Guild of Great Britain with a New Writing Encouragement Award in 2011. Previously, Natalie was Assistant Director at 7:84 Scotland and Associate Director at the New Vic Theatre, Newcastle-under-Lyme, before embarking on a busy freelance career, encompassing theatre productions, live events, actor training and community engagement. She also co-founded Truant Company to produce new LGBTQ+ plays.

Her directing credits include: *The Muddy Choir*, *Twist*, *Advice for the Young at Heart*, *Rise Up*, *The Day the Waters Came* and *Rigged* (all for Theatre Centre), *Smilin' Through* (Truant Co/Birmingham Rep/Contact), *Stigmata* (Truant Co), *Beautiful Thing* (Nottingham Playhouse), *Amy's View* (Salisbury Playhouse), *Brighton Beach Memoirs* (Oldham Coliseum), *Cut to the Chase* (Complete Productions) and *Martha Loves Michael* (Ruffian Productions/Pleasance).

Alice Hallifax | Designer

Alice graduated from Nottingham Trent University with a first class honours degree in Theatre Design. She was the Resident Design Assistant at the Donmar Warehouse in 2017/2018 where she worked on *The Way of the World* (Designer: Anna Fleischle), *The Prime of Miss Jean Brodie* (Designer: Lizzie Clachan), *Aristocrats* (Designer: Es Devlin) and *Measure for Measure* (Designer: Peter McKintosh). Alice is multi-lingual and has worked on productions in Spain and Mexico.

Her previous design credits include: *Pickle Jar* (SOHO Theatre), *Donmar on Design* (Donmar Warehouse Offices), *Recipes from my Grandmother's Kitchen* (Site specific), *The Level of Being* (Nottingham Actors Studio), *Santa Joana dels Escorxadors* (Teatre Alegria), *Electra* (Institut del Teatre).

Ted Barnes | Composer

Ted is a multi-instrumentalist, songwriter, composer and maker. Best known for his work with British songwriter Beth Orton, Ted co-wrote, recorded and played live with Beth for over ten years. As well as releasing three critically acclaimed solo albums he also formed the band 'Clayhill' with long term collaborator Ali Friend (Red Snapper) and the late Gavin Clark (Sunhouse). Through this songwriting partnership he has provided soundtrack material for the films of Shane Meadows from *Dead Man's Shoes* to *This is England.* Alongside writing and producing commercial library albums, Ted can presently be found collaborating with songwriters such as Emily Barker, playing in the *Mrs H and the Sing-along Band* (a much loved family music show), soundtracking for circus companies Extraordinary Bodies and Mimbre, composing theatre soundtracks and devising and performing children's theatre for the National Theatre, London.

Neill Brinkworth | Lighting Designer

Neill trained in Visual Performance and Theatre at Dartington College of Arts. He was nominated for the OffWestEnd Award for Best Lighting Design in 2013 and 2015.

Recent work includes: *Dark Sublime* (Trafalgar Studios), *The Dark* (Fuel Theatre), *The Firm* (Hampstead Theatre), *Blank* (NT Connections, Dorfmann Theatre), *Billy The Kid* (NYMT, Leicester Curve), *Everybody's Talking About Jamie* (Apollo, West End – Associate LD), *Hansel & Gretl* (ROH – Associate LD), *Broadway Showtunes* (Bournemouth Pavillions), *In the Night Garden Live* (Minor Entertainment/BBC), *Lohengrin* – revival (National Opera of Greece, Polish National Opera), *The Meeting* (Hampstead Theatre), *Tamburlaine* (Yellow Earth), *The Cutting of the Cloth* (Southwark Playhouse), *Children of Killers* (NT Connections, Olivier Theatre), *Dido & Aeneas* (English Touring Opera), *As Is* (Trafalgar Studios), *Symbionts* (Wayne McGregor, Estonia National Ballet), *Sweat Factory* (YMT, Sadlers Wells), *Dessa Rose* (Trafalgar Studios), *Vincent River* (Old Vic productions), *The Seagull* (Arcola Theatre), *The Battle of the Boat* (NYMT, Kingston Rose), *Lysistrata, Antigone, Prometheus* (all Cambridge Arts Theatre) and *Step 9 of 12 Tape* (Trafalgar Studios).

Ingrid Mackinnon | Movement Director

Ingrid is a movement director, choreographer, teacher and dancer. She holds an MA in Movement: Directing & Teaching from Royal Central School of Speech and Drama.

Movement direction credits include: *Liar Heretic Thief* (Lyric), *Cacophony* (Almeida), *#WeAreArrested* (RSC), *#DR@CULA!* (RCSSD), *Kingdom Come* (RSC), *Fantastic Mr. Fox* (associate movement Nuffield Southampton and National/International Tour).

Choreography and rehearsal direction credits include: *The Headwrap Diaries* (assistant choreographer and rehearsal director), *Our Mighty Groove* (rehearsal director), *Hansel and Gretel* (assistant choreographer and rehearsal director) for Uchenna Dance, *In The Heights* (choreographer), *Three Penny Opera (choreographer), Imoinda* (choreographer) for Wac Arts and *Boy Breaking Glass* (rehearsal director) for Vocab Dance/ Alesandra Seutin.

Sarah Dickenson | Dramaturg

Sarah's roles include: Associate Dramaturg for LAMDA, Associate Dramaturg for the RSC, Production Dramaturg for the Globe, Senior Reader at Soho Theatre, Literary Manager for Theatre503, New Writing Associate at The Red Room and Founding Coordinator for the South West New Writing Network.

Sarah has worked on performance projects and artistic development nationally and internationally for a wide range of organisations and theatre makers including: Theatre Centre, National Theatre, Bristol Old Vic, Theatre Bristol, Old Vic New Voices, Liverpool Everyman, Champloo, Theatre Royal Bath, Plymouth Theatre Royal, Tamasha, Apples and Snakes, Almeida Theatre, Hall for Cornwall, The Fence and Churchill Theatre.

Faith Austin | Production Manager

Faith has worked in many areas of performance, events, festivals and theatre. Credits include: *Rotterdam* (Hartshorn – Hook), *Red Riding Hood and the Wolf* and *Sleepyhead* (Little Angel Theatre), *Great Odds* (Mac's Arcadian), Pam Ann and Omid Djalili (Bound & Gagged Comedy), *Broadwick Live* and *Ground Control* as well as Field Day, Mighty Hoopla, Truck Festival, Y Not?, Lost Village Festival, Brighton Pride and many others. Faith is currently the Technical & Production Manager for Half Moon Young People's Theatre.

Rob Browning | Company Stage Manager

Rob's theatre stage management credits include: *Icarus* (Unicorn Theatre), *Rosencrantz & Guildenstern are Dead*, *The Divide* (The Old Vic, London), *Hedda Gabler*, *Aladdin* (Salisbury Playhouse), *Suddenly Last Summer*, *The Lady of the Lake*, *Fallen Angels*, *Watch it Sailor!*, *Dial M for Murder*, *Iron*, *Handbagged*, *As You Like it*, *Rails*, *Single Spies*, *Sense & Sensibility* (Theatre by the Lake), *The Arrivals*, *The Sloe Pickers*, *Moominland Midwinter*, *Rumpelstiltskin* (the egg, Theatre Royal Bath), *The Wizard of Oz* (Taunton Brewhouse).

THEATRE
CENTRE

Theatre Centre takes brilliant plays and projects to young people, wherever they are. Our productions present big ideas and difficult questions which can help young audiences make sense of a complex and changing world. We use the power of stories, writing and performance to support students and teachers in their learning across a range of subjects to build confidence and aspiration. Our vision is that children and young people are empowered in their activism and leadership through theatre, using their voices and ideas to make change in themselves and the world around them.

Theatre Centre is a registered charity, and a National Portfolio Organisation supported by Arts Council England.

'Companies like Theatre Centre defy clichés.'
The Guardian

'I have long admired Theatre Centre's work in producing fine plays for young audiences and doing everything possible to promote the genre through new writing.'
The Stage

'Theatre Centre productions bring relevant issues alive through drama to perhaps the most challenging of age groups in a vibrant way that doesn't oversimplify or patronise, but engages them.'
Teacher, Sevenoaks School

For Schools

Want to extend the learning beyond our shows? All our productions support the National Curriculum across a range of subjects. Visit our website to find learning resources for each of our productions, and to dive into our extensive archive:

www.theatre-centre.org.uk/for-schools

Follow us
Website: www.theatre-centre.co.uk
Facebook: facebook.com/TheatreCentreUK
Twitter: @TCLive #TheBorder
Instagram: @theatrecentre #TheBorder

For general enquiries or tour bookings please get in touch on
admin@theatre-centre.co.uk | 020 7729 3066

Reg. Office
Hanover House
14 Hanover Square
London
W1S 1HP

www.theatre-centre.co.uk
Company No: 0585723 (England & Wales)
Charity No: 210262

SWITCHED ON

Teachers, are you planning your PSHE sessions? Looking for current and relevant resources? At Theatre Centre, we're as keen as you to see PSHE become an essential part of education, whilst making it as simple as possible for you to deliver. Switched ON, our series of PSHE toolkits, is designed to help teachers provide successful and engaging lessons at an affordable price. Topics in the series include Mental Health, SRE (Consent) and Online Safety, with our newest toolkit focusing on Financial Resilience coming early 2020.

Our acclaimed Switched ON PSHE teaching toolkits, each centering around a newly commissioned audio play, can be purchased for £49.99 each or only £124.99 for the whole set*. With compulsory SRE approaching, the toolkits provide a framework for sensitive discussion and lesson plans that guide students to explore their own solutions to some of life's harder questions in a safe and responsible way.

Visit our shop to buy yours today: theatre-centre.myshopify.com

*To redeem our whole-set offer, use the code PSHESET at the checkout. If you'd like any more information before buying please get in touch with Joe, Switched ON Co-ordinator, on Joseph@theatre-centre.co.uk.

THE BORDER

Afsaneh Gray

THE BORDER

OBERON BOOKS
LONDON

WWW.OBERONBOOKS.COM

First published in 2019 by Oberon Books Ltd
521 Caledonian Road, London N7 9RH
Tel: +44 (0) 20 7607 3637 / Fax: +44 (0) 20 7607 3629
e-mail: info@oberonbooks.com
www.oberonbooks.com

PB ISBN: 9781786827739
E ISBN: 9781786828163

Cover design by Matt Hodges Design

Visit www.oberonbooks.com to read more about all our books and to buy them. You will
also find features, author interviews and news of any author events, and you can sign up
for e-newsletters and be the first to hear about our new releases.

10 9 8 7 6 5 4 3 2 1

Characters

JULIA: 13 years old

MOTHER: Julia's mother

FATHER: Julia's father

GRANDMA: Julia's grandmother
(FATHER's mother)

STRANGER: A cockapoo

REFUGEE BOY

FEMALE BORDERGUARD

MALE BORDERGUARD

JOGGER

SMUGGLER

MAYOR

CALL CENTRE BOSS

JOURNALIST

/ indicates the point of interruption in overlapping dialogue

… indicates a non-verbal response

Note on the set and character transitions

The set should be bare bones – the minimum necessary to tell
the story effectively. Character transitions should be obvious
and, again, can be minimal. Actors should never leave the
playing space except when specified.

When the actor playing MAYOR breaks with her role, she
should enter the real world as it currently exists outside
the playing space. Changes to the script should be made as
necessary to reflect this.

SONG FOR STRANGER

In the past, long long ago
There was wilderness here
No houses, no fences
Squirrels and freedom
But no humans to clean up your shit
That was in the past
Long, long ago

In the past, less long ago
There was a war here
Sirens and bomb blasts,
Death and starvation
And humans who'd dine out on dog
That was in the past
Long, long ago

In the past, yesterday
There was a park here
No houses, no fences
Squirrels and freedom
Plus humans to clean up your shit
That was in the past
Long, long ago

How do I know this?
I know this because I'm a dog
I can see into the past
I can see into the future
Why?
Because I'm a dog

In the past, earlier today
There was a fence here
A border for humans
West Oolians, East Oolians
Nations split like species of dog
That's not in the past
Long, long ago

In which Julia tries to persuade her family to help her find her dog.

Monday evening.

Dinner time.

GRANDMA, MOTHER and FATHER are sat around the dinner table. JULIA stands.

JULIA: Mum –

MOTHER: Sit down / Julia

JULIA: But Mum –

FATHER: What's for dinner?
　　Smells wonderful.

MOTHER: Your favourite.

JULIA: Mum, Stranger –

MOTHER: Julia, your father's waiting –

JULIA: But listen –

MOTHER: You know we all sit down and eat together in this
　　family –

FATHER: Poppet, listen to your mother.
　　I'm starving…

JULIA: But Stranger's gone!

　　Beat.

MOTHER: You lost the dog?

JULIA: I didn't lose her! One minute she was right in front of
　　me – I mean, I let her off the leash but I always do that in
　　the dog park – but then she saw a squirrel and ran after it
　　and then – and then there was this fence –

5

FATHER: Sorry, which dog?

MOTHER: We got it for her Terry!

FATHER: Did we?

MOTHER: To teach her personal responsibility.

FATHER: Ah yes. Good.
    Is anybody going to dish out the stew?

GRANDMA: I always said pets bring nothing but grief…
    One minute they're there, the next minute they're dead –

JULIA: She's not dead, Grandma! And it's not her fault they
    closed the border!

Beat.

GRANDMA: They what, / dear?

FATHER: They what?

JULIA: They put a fence up in the middle of the dog park.
    Along the line that marks the border between East and
    West Oolia.

Beat.

GRANDMA: I don't believe it.

MOTHER: My God.

FATHER: They wouldn't…

GRANDMA: There must be some mistake –

JULIA: That's what I'm telling you! That's where Stranger is.
    On the other side of the fence – in West Oolia.

MOTHER: I knew the mayor was a woman of her word…

JULIA:	Mum!
FATHER:	Tina!
GRANDMA:	Tina!

MOTHER: Sorry! But it's nice to see my vote count for once – it's nice to feel listened to.

FATHER: You didn't mean it when you voted for her. It was a protest vote.

MOTHER: I did mean it.

FATHER: Then you're an idiot!

MOTHER: Excuse me?

FATHER: You have no idea what this is going to do to the garage...

MOTHER: I don't know about the garage, but I know it's going to protect my job...

GRANDMA: Grandpa's heart would break if he were alive to see this...

JULIA: What about Stranger?

MOTHER: Love, I'm sure your dog will come back...

GRANDMA: Of course, it already broke – poor man died of a heart attack –

JULIA: She can't! I told you! There's a stupid fence in the way!

GRANDMA: But he'll be turning in his grave – East and West Oolia divided / again –

FATHER: Dogs and dead people are the least of our worries!

JULIA takes out her phone.

MOTHER: Phone, Julia.

7

NEW POST FROM @JULIAFROMEASTOOLIA: MY
DOG STRANGER IS MISSING. LAST SEEN ON
THE WEST OOLIAN SIDE OF THE DOG PARK –

FATHER: Julia! You know the rule. Not at table.

JULIA puts her phone away reluctantly.

FATHER: Isn't anyone going to dish out the stew?

MOTHER: Why don't you do it?

I cooked it, despite working all day for minimum wage!

FATHER: I paid for the ingredients –

MOTHER: No you didn't. I'm the one who pays for the food
on this table –

FATHER: Well I paid for the table! For the whole kitchen in fact!

GRANDMA: Strictly speaking, this is my house you're living
in…

*FATHER tries to grab the pot, MOTHER snatches it away from him.
They have a tug of war which ends with MOTHER tipping the pot
over FATHER's head.*

A breath.

FATHER removes the pot and attempts to regain his dignity.

FATHER licks his lips.

FATHER: Can somebody pass me a spoon?

JULIA passes FATHER a spoon. He tucks in.

MOTHER: You know, greed is not an attractive quality…

GRANDMA: *(To JULIA.)* Have I ever told you how me and
Grandpa met, dear?

JULIA: Like a million times, Grandma

8

FATHER: Neither is small-minded bigotry!

MOTHER: If I'm a bigot, so is the majority of East Oolia!

MOTHER snatches the pot and spoon from FATHER and eats the stew.

GRANDMA: He was a soldier in the war and when peace was
declared he was posted to the border. Now, I wanted some
honey for a honey cake but we were all out and I'd heard
they still had some in West Oolia. I went to the border and
I saw your grandpa – handsome man – and I said to him
'if you let me cross I'll bring you a slice of my cake'. Of
course, as he always said, he couldn't resist either the cake
or me…

JULIA: I know, Grandma.

GRANDMA: But when he came to live here I said to him,
I said Jeffrey the neighbours will talk. You coming from
West Oolia. And he said to me, don't worry Sylvia, they'll
come round. A stranger is just a friend you haven't made
yet.

JULIA: That's why Stranger's called Stranger.

GRANDMA: You go down to the border, my girl. You tell
them you won't let their fence get in the way of two
friends. Much better than all this socializing media.

JULIA: Social media

GRANDMA: Instead of that, you talk to them face to face.
That park's called Peace Park for a reason. They put it
right there, in between East and West Oolia where no
man's land was during the war. Your grandpa –

JULIA: This isn't about Grandpa, Grandma.

FATHER: That's right. It's about –

JULIA: No. It's not about any of you. It's about my dog.

JULIA picks up her phone and gets up.

MOTHER: Julia –

JULIA: No!

I'm not hungry.

JULIA leaves the table.

Monday evening, 8pm.

@JULIAFROMEASTOOLIA POSTS A PICTURE OF HER BELOVED COCKAPOO STRANGER. SHE APPEARS TO BE JUMPING FOR A BALL. IN FACT, SHE'S CONSIDERING THE PROFOUND EFFECT OF GRAVITY ON HIERARCHIES AND THE WAY WE RELATE TO EACH OTHER.

@JULIAFROMEASTOOLIA POSTS A PICTURE OF STRANGER AND COMMENTS: HELP! MY DOG STRANGER IS MISSING! LAST SEEN IN THE DOG PARK, ON THE #WESTOOLIAN SIDE. CAN'T GET HOME BECAUSE OF THE #CLOSEDBORDER. IS WEARING A COLLAR. DOG EMOJI. SAD FACE EMOJI. #DOGSOFEASTOOLIA

FIVE LIKES

ONE SHARE

@IHEARTDOGS: CUTE DOG.

SCENE TWO

In which Julia tries to get across to West Oolia to find Stranger.

The next morning.

The border at the dog park. FEMALE BORDERGUARD and MALE BORDERGUARD are guarding the fence.

A JOGGER enters, and approaches the border. Tries to get across.

FEMALE BORDERGUARD: Go round.

JOGGER: But –

FEMALE BORDERGUARD: Go round.

>*JOGGER tries to run across the line of the border.*

FEMALE BORDERGUARD: Not that way! Back the way you came.

>*JOGGER runs back in a semi-circle. Continues to do this.*

>*JULIA approaches.*

JULIA: I want to go to West Oolia, please.

FEMALE BORDERGUARD: Passport.

>*JULIA hands FEMALE BORDERGUARD her passport. She looks at the picture.*

FEMALE BORDERGUARD: Lol.

JULIA: …

FEMALE BORDERGUARD: Everyone always looks like a drug dealer in these photos.

JULIA: I'm thirteen.

>*FEMALE BORDERGUARD gives it back.*

JULIA: Can I cross? I'll be late for school –

FEMALE BORDERGUARD: Wrong passport.

JULIA: But I only just got it –

FEMALE BORDERGUARD: East Oolia has issued new
passports. Pink, not blue.
There was an announcement yesterday. After the mayor
closed the border.

JULIA: Does that mean I have to get another one?

FEMALE BORDERGUARD: Don't worry, it's all automatic.

JULIA: So where is it?

FEMALE BORDERGUARD: Stuck in West Oolia.

JULIA: …

FEMALE BORDERGUARD: The contract was awarded to a
West Oolian company. West Oolia's just more efficient like
that. We're a West Oolian company.
I'm West Oolian.

JULIA: But you're guarding the East Oolian border…

FEMALE BORDERGUARD: Our official title is Separation
Enforcers. We mostly build fences. We can build a fence
in just under 23 minutes and 30 seconds. It's all flat pack
from Swedeway.

JULIA: I just want to get to the other side of the dog park –
I'll be like five minutes –

FEMALE BORDERGUARD: No can do. With the border closed
and no trade agreement your passport's stuck, like I said.

JULIA: But my dog's over there!

FEMALE BORDERGUARD: Dog?

Dogs are no business of ours. They come and go as they like.

JULIA: They don't come and go as they like 'cause you've built a fence in the middle of the dog park!

FEMALE BORDERGUARD: Don't get aggressive with me...

JULIA: It's not aggression it's not aggression it's frust – frust –

JOGGER, who happens to be passing at this point, knows exactly what JULIA means...

JOGGER: Frustration?

JULIA: Yes!

JOGGER goes back to her semi-circles.

JULIA: *(To MALE BORDERGUARD.)* Can you help?

MALE BORDERGUARD: She's the boss.

JULIA: Are there borderguards in the playground as well?

FEMALE BORDERGUARD: Separation Enforcers.

JULIA: And I obviously can't use the jogging track...

FEMALE BORDERGUARD: ...

JULIA: The boating lake?

FEMALE BORDERGUARD: Closed.

MALE BORDERGUARD: Except migrants keep sneaking over on pedalos and then falling in because pedalos only hold two people or four at / a stretch –

FEMALE BORDERGUARD: Shhh!

MALE BORDERGUARD: Not for much longer. We're working on it.

Beat.

JULIA: Can you at least tell me if you've seen her then? She's about so big, brown wavy fur, cute button nose. Cockapoo. She / was –

FEMALE BORDERGUARD points her gun at JULIA.

FEMALE BORDERGUARD: GET BACK GET BACK GET BACK!

JOGGER crouches in terror.

MALE BORDERGUARD: Er, boss? It's a breed. It's a cross between / a cocker spaniel and a –

FEMALE BORDERGUARD: I'll thank you to keep your language clean! Both of you!

JULIA: If she dies out here, it's your fault!

FEMALE BORDERGUARD: Do I look like I care?

JULIA turns and walks away. JOGGER exits, terrified.

MALE BORDERGUARD sticks up his hand.

MALE BORDERGUARD: I need a wazz.

FEMALE BORDERGUARD: …

MALE BORDERGUARD: It's in my contract that / I get –

FEMALE BORDERGUARD: Two minute bathroom break. That's it.

MALE BORDERGUARD goes to JULIA. FEMALE BORDERGUARD starts ostentatiously counting two minutes.

FEMALE BORDERGUARD: One Mississippi, two Mississippi….

MALE BORDERGUARD: I've got a dog myself. A Shih Tzu.

JULIA: …

MALE BORDERGUARD: It's a breed.

JULIA: Yeah I know what it is.

MALE BORDERGUARD: Word of advice – there are gangs of migrant kids in the neighbourhood. Stealing dogs.

JULIA: What? Why?

MALE BORDERGUARD: Sell 'em.

JULIA: She's not been stolen, she's just over there, on the other side of the fence!

MALE BORDERGUARD: That's what you think.

Cockapoos are like gold dust. Migrants are grabbing them any chance they get.

JULIA: …

MALE BORDERGUARD: Most of the dog breeding happens in East Oolia, see? We're big dog breeders. So with the border closed, dogs can't get through. West Oolians are so faddish. Couple of years ago it was all cats and now it's all dogs, all #meandmycockapoo.

I'm East Oolian.

FEMALE BORDERGUARD: One minute thirty seconds Mississippi, one minute thirty-one / seconds Mississippi!

MALE BORDERGUARD: So if I was on the hunt for a missing dog, I'd start there.

JULIA: But –

MALE BORDERGUARD: Oh piss I really do need a wazz!

FEMALE BORDERGUARD: One minute, FIFTY-NINE seconds Mississippi –

MALE BORDERGUARD: Good luck finding your cockapee –
I mean poo – I mean – oh piss!

*MALE BORDERGUARD runs back to the border before JULIA has a
chance to ask...*

JULIA: But where do I find a migrant?!

SCENE THREE

In which Julia meets a migrant and accuses him
of stealing her dog.

Later that day.

*JULIA is returning home from school when she sees REFUGEE BOY. He
looks wet and dishevelled.*

JULIA: Hey!

REFUGEE BOY: ...

JULIA: What are you doing outside my house?

REFUGEE BOY: I didn't know I was.

JULIA: Why are you all wet?

REFUGEE BOY: I had a shower.

JULIA: In your clothes?

REFUGEE BOY: ...

JULIA: Are you a migrant?

REFUGEE BOY: No.

JULIA takes out her phone.

REFUGEE BOY: What are you doing?

JULIA: Yeah you are. That's why you're all wet. You tried to sneak across the boating lake in a pedalo but you fell in because pedalos only hold two people –

REFUGEE BOY: Who are you calling?

JULIA: The police!

REFUGEE BOY: But I'm not a migrant, I'm a refugee!

JULIA: What's the difference?

REFUGEE BOY: I'm fleeing persecution. I'm not a bad person – there's war in my country. That's why I had to leave.

JULIA: I don't know what's going on in your country but there's no war in West Oolia. You could have just stayed there.

REFUGEE BOY: People in West Oolia spit on migrants – refugees – on the street. East Oolians aren't like that.

JULIA: …

REFUGEE BOY: My mum told me stories about East Oolia. She said the people were friendly and the fruit grows on trees by the side of the road for anyone to pick…

JULIA: I mean the fruit here's alright, but we get it from the supermarket, same as everyone else.

REFUGEE BOY: …

JULIA: I'll show you if you want.

JULIA turns to go into the house.

REFUGEE BOY: Can I come in?

JULIA: No!
I don't know you. You can wait here.

REFUGEE BOY: I just… I noticed you have a dog bowl and –

JULIA: So you are a migrant!

REFUGEE BOY: What? No I'm –

JULIA: I know migrants are stealing dogs! But mine's already
    gone, so don't bother…

REFUGEE BOY: Oh!
    I'm sorry.
    I have a dog at home. Dogs don't judge you – they just
    love you.

    Beat.

JULIA: I'll get you the fruit and then I want you to go.

    JULIA goes into the house and comes back with some fruit.

JULIA: It's my grandma's.
    She doesn't want it.

REFUGEE BOY: It's from the supermarket.

JULIA: I told you.

    Beat.

JULIA: If you see my dog, will you tell me? She's a cockapoo
    – brown wavy hair, cute button nose. Apparently, they're
    really valuable. She's called Stranger – she's got a collar on.

    Beat.

REFUGEE BOY: In my language the word for Stranger is the
    same as the word for friend.

SOCIAL MEDIA INTERLUDE 2

Tuesday afternoon, 4pm.

@JULIAFROMEASTOOLIA POSTS A PICTURE
OF HER BELOVED COCKAPOO STRANGER.
SHE SEEMS TO BE LOOKING UP AT JULIA
AND BEGGING. IN FACT, SHE'S WONDERING
IF WE CAN EVER ESCAPE INEQUALITY AND
HEGELIAN MASTER/SLAVE DIALECTICS AS
LONG AS SOME PEOPLE HAVE ALL THE TREATS.

@JULIAFROMEASTOOLIA: KEEP YOUR
DOGS SAFE INDOORS! #DOGSOFEASTOOLIA
#BETTERSAFETHANSORRY #STILLMISSING

TWENTY-THREE LIKES

FIVE SAD FACE EMOJIS

@IHEARTDOGS: SHARE

SCENE FOUR

In which Julia tries to hide the fate of Grandma's fruit.

The next morning. Breakfast.

GRANDMA is looking in her cupboard.

FATHER is sitting at the table with nothing in front of him, dejected and confused.

MOTHER is getting her stuff together for work.

JULIA is eating cereal.

GRANDMA: Has anyone seen my fruit?

MOTHER: Julia, tell your father that if he wants breakfast, he
    can get it himself.

FATHER: I can't do anything in this fragile economy…

MOTHER: I can't stomach breakfast, not since I heard the news.

GRANDMA: I always keep it in my cupboard…

JULIA: What news?

MOTHER: People like your father have kicked up a fuss,
    so the mayor's called a debate at the Town Hall about
    whether the border stays closed. Then there's going to be
    a vote. So much for democracy!

FATHER: A vote *is* democracy!

MOTHER: You can't just keep asking people the same
    question until you get the answer you want!

FATHER: Poppet, what are you eating?

GRANDMA: I was keeping a few punnets to take back to the
    supermarket.

MOTHER: Grandma, you've got to stop doing this…

FATHER: *(To JULIA.)* Looks tasty…

JULIA: Have some, Dad!

JULIA gives FATHER the cereal.

MOTHER: Of course, he can't resist filling his belly…

FATHER: Tell your mother I always get a headache if I don't eat. Where's the milk?

GRANDMA: Are you sure no one's seen it?

JULIA gives FATHER the milk.

FATHER: What about the bowls?

JULIA's phone gets an alert. She checks it.

MOTHER: Julia – we're having breakfast –

JULIA: But someone commented on my post, they might have some news about Stranger…

@DOGGONEBAD TO
@JULIAFROMEASTOOLIA: SECOND
THIS – KEEP YOUR DOGS INDOORS
FOLKS. MY DOG WAS TAKEN LAST NIGHT.
BORDER COLLIE. #DOGSOFEASTOOLIA
#BETTERSAFETHANSORRY

@JULIAFROMEASTOOLIA TO @DOGGONEBAD:
SAD FACE.

MOTHER: I don't care. After breakfast.

FATHER: Poppet. A bowl?

JULIA is about to put her phone away when she gets another alert.

@COCKAWHODAMAN TO @JULIAFROMEASTOOLIA
AND @DOGGONEBAD: MY COCKAPOO WENT
MISSING LAST NIGHT!! #DOGSOFEASTOOLIA
#BETTERSAFETHANSORRY #CLOSEDBORDERS
#MIGRANTSOUT

MOTHER: Julia –

JULIA: But –

FATHER: But what? I can't eat cereal without a bowl!

GRANDMA: Julia, dear, have *you* seen my fruit?

JULIA gets FATHER a bowl. He pours himself some cereal.

GRANDMA: Julia?

JULIA: I gave your fruit to a refugee, Grandma!

GRANDMA: But you knew I was saving it to take back to the
supermarket!

JULIA: Yeah and they must think you're mad!

GRANDMA: I don't care if they do! They have to learn that
their fruit doesn't taste of anything!

MOTHER: When did you meet a refugee?

JULIA: He said there was a war in his country. He looked
hungry.

Beat.

GRANDMA: Well at least it went to someone who needed it.

FATHER: Yes, that's very generous of you poppet. Very
inclusive. Of course, your mother won't think so.
Spoon?

JULIA gets FATHER a spoon.

JULIA: I don't think he was a bad person, Mum.

MOTHER: If he really was a refugee, I don't mind you helping him. I'm actually very generous, unlike your father.

FATHER: I'm generous!

MOTHER: } Ha!

GRANDMA: } Ha!

FATHER: Generous spirited.

JULIA: What's the difference between a migrant and a refugee, Grandma?

GRANDMA: A migrant is someone who leaves their country out of choice, dear – for whatever reason – and a refugee is forced out. Because of war, for example, like your friend.

MOTHER: The only reason your father likes migrants is 'cause he gets away with paying them less than he would an East Oolian.

FATHER: Nonsense!

GRANDMA: Was he good-looking, this refugee boy of yours?

JULIA: Ew Grandma no.

GRANDMA: I wasn't much older than you when I met Grandpa.

FATHER: Mother, you heard her, he's ugly!

JULIA's phone gets an alert. She checks her phone.

@EASTOOLIANPATRIOT TO @JULIAFROMEASTOOLIA, @DOGGONEBAD AND @COCKAWHODAMAN: THREE DOGS MISSING IN THREE DAYS. BLACK BAME WHATEVER YOU WANT TO CALL PEOPLE WITH A FUNNY TINGE ALL OVER EAST OOLIA.

COINCIDENCE? THINK NOT. #DOGSOFEASTOOLIA
#CLOSEDBORDERS #MIGRANTSOUT

@COCKAWHODAMAN: SHARE.

SHARE. SHARE. SHARE. SHARE. SHARE.

MOTHER: Julia – don't make me say it again –

JULIA: But are migrants bad then?

FATHER: No, they're just trying to build a better life for
themselves –

MOTHER: At the expense of our lives –

GRANDMA: There's room for everybody, surely –

MOTHER: It doesn't always feel like there's room for me!

JULIA's phone gets an alert. She checks it.

@MAYOROFEASTOOLIA SHARES
@JULIAFROMEASTOOLIA'S POST.

SHE POSTS A PICTURE OF TWO JACK RUSSELL
TERRIERS. THEY SEEM TO BE EACH LICKING
ONE OF HER HANDS. IN FACT, THEY'RE
THINKING ABOUT THE DOUBLE-SIDED NATURE
OF EVERYTHING IN LIFE, WHEREBY TWO
HANDS CAN LOOK SIMILAR AND YET TASTE
DIFFERENT DEPENDING ON WHICH HAND WAS
USED TO HOLD THE ONION AND WHICH TO
HOLD THE KNIFE.

@MAYOROFEASTOOLIA COMMENTS: SO SORRY
TO HEAR THIS @JULIAFROMEASTOOLIA.
I HAVE TWO DOGS MYSELF, RIGHTIE
AND LEFTIE. #DOGSOFEASTOOLIA
#BETTERSAFETHANSORRY

10....20......30...........50.....................85 LIKES
63 SHARES 32 THUMBS UP 21 LOVE HEARTS
12 SAD FACES 1 LOL.

MOTHER: / Julia!

JULIA: Woah…

JULIA gets up.

JULIA: I'm going to school.

MOTHER: You haven't finished your breakfast –

JULIA: I don't want it.

MOTHER takes JULIA's phone.

MOTHER: That's it! It's confiscated!

JULIA: But – you don't understand – the mayor just shared my
post about / Stranger –

MOTHER: Confiscated.

Beat.

JULIA: The mayor cares more about my dog than you do.

SCENE FIVE

In which Refugee Boy tries to get his brother out of West Oolia.

Wednesday afternoon. The SMUGGLER's house.

*REFUGEE BOY knocks on the door. SMUGGLER takes a while to answer.
Looks shifty when she does.*

SMUGGLER: What are you doing here? You'll get me into
trouble.

REFUGEE BOY: Have you sold the dog yet?

SMUGGLER: What dog?

REFUGEE BOY: It was swimming across the lake and I jumped in and got it?

SMUGGLER: Er…

REFUGEE BOY: Don't you remember me?

SMUGGLER: You all look the same, to be honest.

REFUGEE BOY: Well that dog is really valuable. It's a poo-a-cock.

SMUGGLER: *(Finding this funny.)* A what now?

REFUGEE BOY: So if you sell it you can bring my brother across. My brother's still in West Oolia. Remember?

SMUGGLER: I'm waiting for the price to go up. Border's only been closed for a couple of days – got to let the market catch up.

Anyway, I would have said two dogs. One for yourself, one for your brother.

REFUGEE BOY: But I'm telling you that one's worth a lot.

SMUGGLER: I'd have said two dogs. Those pedalos don't come cheap.

REFUGEE BOY: But I looked for another dog where the first one came from and she only had one.

SMUGGLER: Listen, boy. You're lucky that the black market in dogs is on the up and up because otherwise it would be money and I know for a fact that you don't have any of that.

Just get me a dog. And if I were you I'd get it quickly, because they're working on that boating lake and before long they'll find a way to build a fence across the middle of that too. The… poo-a-cocks!

REFUGEE BOY: …

SMUGGLER: Oh, and your brother gave me a message for you.

Let me see if I can remember what it was…

Oh yeah.

Help.

SMUGGLER slams the door in REFUGEE BOY's face.

SOCIAL MEDIA INTERLUDE 5

Wednesday afternoon, 5pm.

@FUNNYTINGE SEARCHES FOR #DOGSOFEASTOOLIA

TOP RESULT:

@MAYOROFESATOOLIA: SO SORRY TO HEAR
THIS @JULIAFROMEASTOOLIA. I HAVE
TWO DOGS MYSELF, RIGHTIE AND LEFTIE.
#DOGSOFEASTOOLIA #BETTERSAFETHANSORRY

@FUNNYTINGE: LIKE.

SCENE SIX

In which Julia tries to persuade the Mayor to help her find Stranger.

Thursday morning.

The MAYOR's office at the Town Hall.

MAYOR shakes hands with JULIA.

MAYOR: @JULIAFROMEASTOOLIA!

JULIA: Just Julia's fine…

MAYOR: I'm so sorry about your dog.

JULIA: Thanks.

MAYOR: Taken by migrants…

JULIA: She might just be stuck in West Oolia to be / fair –

MAYOR: I love dogs. Have two.

JULIA: Yeah. I saw your / post –

MAYOR: Yes everyone likes dogs, don't they? They're so relatable.
   Except for people who like cats. Do you like cats?

JULIA: Erm, yeah, / I –

MAYOR: I've got a couple of them, too. I draw the line at the
   weirder animals.
   Monkeys. Ferrets. Snakes.

JULIA: …

MAYOR: So.
   Tell me about your dog.

JULIA: So she's called Stranger and / she's a –

MAYOR: Stranger? Unusual.

JULIA: It's because she was a rescue dog and when I first met her
    she was a stranger but I knew she was just a friend I / hadn't –

MAYOR: What about Fido, or… Buster?

JULIA: …

MAYOR: Something more normal.

JULIA: It's her name.

MAYOR: Strong-minded! How exciting.
    Well I'm looking forward to you speaking at the Town
    Hall, anyway. Young people always get edited into little
    clips and shared. It's such fun.

JULIA: The Town Hall?

MAYOR: That is why you're here isn't it?

JULIA: Er, actually I thought maybe I could just go to West
    Oolia and put up some posters? See if anyone's seen / her?

MAYOR: But the border's closed.

JULIA: Yeah but you're the mayor, so can't / you –

MAYOR: 'Yeah'… and I closed it.
    Besides, we're currently having a little issue with passports.

JULIA: …

MAYOR: I know, it's daunting. Getting up in front of people.
    Speaking. I was never really the type to put myself
    forward either. It was just what was expected of me.
    And now the people of East Oolia expect something of
    you, Julia.

JULIA: I don't think they do – I'm / just –

MAYOR: Oh yes! Let's see…

MAYOR takes out her phone.

30

MAYOR: Just in the last couple of minutes…

@SCHMUCKFORASCHNAUZER: HEARTBROKEN.
MY DOG'S GONE. KEPT HIM INDOORS BUT
SOME THIEVES BROKE IN. #CLOSEDBORDERS

I like this one's username…

@TAKEBACKCOLLIETROL – See what they did there?
Very good.

NGL, I'M NOT MEAN AND I'M NOT RACIST BUT
MIGRANTS ARE TAKING DOGS. ALSO, SOME
OF MY BEST FRIENDS ARE FROM ABROAD.
#CLOSEDBORDERS

I could go on.

You're a hero of the #closedborders movement.

Beat.

JULIA: So that's why you want me to speak?

MAYOR: I want you to speak because I believe young people
deserve to be heard.

JULIA: Really?

MAYOR: Okay, yes, 'for reals' – I also think your story illustrates
why East Oolia is safer with the border closed. Don't you?

JULIA: I don't know what I think about the border.

MAYOR: But your dog was taken by migrants.

JULIA: You keep saying that but I don't know if it's true.

Beat.

MAYOR: Well, it was good meeting you anyway – good luck
finding your dog – of course, publicity always helps but I'm
sure you could try… oo, I don't know – those posters perhaps?

31

JULIA: Wait!

MAYOR: …

JULIA: What if I just speak about Stranger? And that's it.

MAYOR: …

JULIA: I can do it.

MAYOR: Convince me.

JULIA: …

   …

   …

MAYOR: I'm not convinced –

JULIA: I'll just say that I lost my dog and I want her back and
other people have lost their dogs too and we need to do
something about it because it's not fair!

Beat.

MAYOR: Alright. You're on.

They shake. A camera flashes.

JULIA leaves.

SCENE SEVEN
In which Julia decides to help Refugee Boy.

A few minutes later.

*JULIA leaves the Town Hall and sees REFUGEE BOY. He is sitting on a
bench in the public square outside, looking for the MAYOR.*

JULIA approaches him.

JULIA: What are you doing here?

REFUGEE BOY: Nothing…

Beat.

JULIA: Have you / seen my dog?

REFUGEE BOY: Are you @JULIAFROMEASTOOLIA?

JULIA: Yeah, / why?

REFUGEE BOY: No, sorry.

Beat.

REFUGEE BOY: The mayor says you're going to speak in
favour of closed borders at the Town Hall.

JULIA: I never said that.

REFUGEE BOY: *(Indicating his phone.)* She says you did.

JULIA: My stupid parents confiscated mine. Can I see?

REFUGEE BOY gives JULIA his phone.

She reads the thread…

@MAYOROFEASTOOLIA POSTS A PHOTOGRAPH
OF HER AND @JULIAFROMEASTOOLIA
SHAKING HANDS WITH THE COMMENT: GREAT
MEETING WITH @JULIAFROMEASTOOLIA.
LOOKING FORWARD TO HEARING HER SPEAK
AT THE #TOWNHALL ABOUT THE IMPORTANCE
OF #CLOSEDBORDERS FOR KEEPING OUR
DOGS SAFE. #DOGSOFEASTOOLIA

3015 LIKES. 3018 LIKES. 4010 LIKES.

JULIA: What?

Dives back in.

@ILOVEFUNNYCATS TO @MAYOROFEASTOOLIA
AND @JULIAFROMEASTOOLIA: WHO IS
GOING TO BE TALKING ABOUT CATS??
#CATSOFEASTOOLIA #INTERSECTIONALITY

@EASTOOLIANPATRIOT: HEAVEN HAS A WALL,
A GATE, AND A STRICT IMMIGRATION POLICY.
HELL HAS OPEN BORDERS...

@IHEARTDOGS ISN'T THIS SUPPOSED TO
BE ABOUT DOGS? CAN WE JUST FOCUS
ON DOGS PLEASE? #DOGSOFEASTOOLIA
#REMEMBERTHEM?

@MSMJOURNOSEATSHIT NO WE CANNOT
FOCUS ON DOGS COS PEOPLE'S LIVES ARE AT
STAKE FROM #OPENBORDERS. I WILL EAT A
DOG IN MY BURGER BUT NOT A PERSON.

@MANSPLAINER LET ME TELL YOU
SOMETHING ABOUT #CLOSEDBORDERS...
WHAT IT IS IS A BORDER THAT'S CLOSED.
THANK YOU FOR LISTENING, WOMENFOLK.

@WOKEBOY BITCH PLS. YOUR DOG'S NOT SAFE
COS OF THE DAMN FENCE THEY PUT UP IN THE
MIDDLE OF THE DOGPARK. NUTTIN TO DO
WITH BROWN/BLACK PPL OR PPL OF 'FUNNY
TINGE'. GET A GRIP.

@HUGABEAR: I LOVE LOVE. I SPREAD LOVE
THROUGH HUGS. IF WE ALL HUGGED MORE THE
WORLD WOULD BE A BETTER AND MORE LOVING
PLACE. I AM HERE @JULIAFROMEASTOOLIA WITH
OPEN ARMS AND #OPENBORDERS

SPONSORED AD: @SECURITYSOLUTIONS: WE
PROVIDE GOOD QUALITY FENCES FOR ALL

YOUR SECURITY NEEDS. #CLOSEDBORDERS #INVESTINSECURITY

JULIA emerges from the thread like she's surfacing from deep water.

JULIA: Oh my God what? I never said that! I said I wasn't going to talk about borders at all…

REFUGEE BOY: Isn't that what the Town Hall's about?

JULIA: And now I've got like a million people following me!

REFUGEE BOY: About whether the border stays closed or not?

JULIA: I mean what do I do? I don't want to talk about the border! It's boring.

Beat.

REFUGEE BOY: My brother's stuck in West Oolia. He can't come across because we don't have the money. He's being kept in a basement with hundreds of other people. Is that boring?

Beat.

JULIA: I don't agree with all the stuff people are saying, by the way. About migrants. I mean, I know you're not a migrant, you're a refugee, but no one knows the difference, so –

REFUGEE BOY: If you don't agree with it then tell them.

JULIA: But –

REFUGEE BOY: But what?

JULIA: I don't know.

It's complicated.

Beat.

REFUGEE BOY: Last night I called my mother. I told her: we're fine. We're in school, doing well. People are friendly here, there's fruit growing on trees by the side of the road. Let me speak to your brother, she said. He's out, I told her, he's studying. So late?

She keeps asking, I keep making excuses. I don't know how many more excuses I can give.

Yesterday someone spat at me on the street. Here, in East Oolia.

Pause.

JULIA: Give me your phone.

REFUGEE BOY does.

JULIA: I'm signing in, okay?

REFUGEE BOY shrugs.

JULIA types something. Hands it back.

REFUGEE BOY types something. Hands the phone back to JULIA.

JULIA: You're @funnytinge?

REFUGEE BOY: …

JULIA: Thanks for liking my post.

REFUGEE: That's a heart. I loved it.

SOCIAL MEDIA INTERLUDE 6

Thursday morning, 9am.

@JULIAFROMEASTOOLIA: THANKS FOR
SHARING YOUR STORIES, EVERYBODY.
FENCES SEPARATE DOGS AND HUMANS FROM
THEIR FAMILIES. MORE COMING UP AT THE
#TOWNHALL ON SUNDAY.

@FUNNYTINGE: LOVE HEART

@TAKEBACKCOLLIETROL: ANGRY FACE

@COCKAWHODAMAN: ANGRY FACE

@EASTOOLIANPATRIOT: ANGRY FACE

@HUGABEAR: LOVE HEART

@MAYOROFEASTOOLIA POSTS A PHOTOGRAPH
OF HER TWO JACK RUSSELL TERRIERS PULLING
AT THE LEASH. THE DOGS SEEM TO BE GLADLY
RUNNING ON AHEAD. IN FACT, THEY ARE
WONDERING WHY THERE MUST ALWAYS BE
LEADERS AND FOLLOWERS, AND WHETHER A
MORE HORIZONTAL POWER STRUCTURE IN
WHICH EVERYONE SEEKS CONSENSUS WILL EVER
BE POSSIBLE.

@MAYOROFEASTOOLIA COMMENTS: MY HEART
IS BROKEN. MY TWO DOGS – RIGHTIE AND
LEFTIE – WERE TAKEN LAST NIGHT. POLICE ARE
LOOKING FOR A GANG OF YOUNG, BEARDED
MEN, PROBABLY NOT EAST OOLIAN. I HAVE
PERSONALLY SENT MYSELF CONDOLENCES.
#KEEPOURDOGSSAFE #CLOSEDBORDERS

SCENE EIGHT

In which Julia tries to get her phone back.

That evening.

Dinner.

MOTHER, FATHER and JULIA are sat around the dinner table.

There's nothing on it.

JULIA: What's for dinner?

MOTHER: Nothing. I'm on strike.

FATHER: 'I'm on strike.'

JULIA: Can I have my phone back / then please?

MOTHER: I work all day for peanuts and then I come home and work for even less. And now the opinion polls show that people want to open the border again. So you can have your open border, but I'm done.

FATHER: 'But I'm done'

MOTHER: Obviously no one listens to what I think, anyway

FATHER: 'No one listens to what I think, anyway'

JULIA: No one listens to anyone in this family!
Mum, can I have my phone back?

MOTHER: Not until after dinner.

JULIA: But there's no food!

MOTHER: Doesn't matter! In this family we eat together.

Beat.

JULIA: Where's Grandma then?

FATHER: I'll tell you where she is. In bed, terrified there's going to be a war again. Of course, she's not wrong…

MOTHER: Don't be ridiculous.

FATHER: Trade war!

MOTHER: 'Trade war.'

JULIA: Mum!

MOTHER: A trade war isn't a real war, love. It's just someone doing something to protect our jobs.

FATHER: 'A trade war isn't a real war'

MOTHER: A trade war *isn't* a real war

FATHER: 'A trade war *isn't* a real war'

MOTHER: It isn't!

FATHER: 'A trade war isn't a real / war'

JULIA: Shut up!

Beat.

MOTHER: Julia –

JULIA: If you want to argue, why don't you do it at the Town Hall debate on Sunday?

MOTHER: I'll be there, of course, / but –

FATHER: So will I –

MOTHER: You can't talk to us like / that –

JULIA: I'm making a speech! At the debate. The mayor said I could.

Beat.

MOTHER: About what?

JULIA: Probably in favour of open borders…

MOTHER: …

JULIA: Mum, I just want things to go back to how they were before the border closed. When Stranger was here and you and Dad didn't argue all day long.

FATHER: You're quite right, poppet. Life was better with the border open.

MOTHER: What about my life? Because if the border opens and the call centre moves, there are going to be a lot more dinners like this.

JULIA: You don't know the call centre's going to move. I'll go there – speak to them –

MOTHER: You don't understand.

JULIA: …

MOTHER: Your dad and grandma, they've benefited from this system their whole life. They own the garage, they own this house… Everything I've ever had I've worked for. I'm not a mean person. I just want something that's mine.

MOTHER gives JULIA her phone.

MOTHER: You can get down.

Thursday evening, 8pm.

@IHEARTDOGS TO @JULIAFROMEASTOOLIA: MY DOG'S GONE NOW TOO! LAB CALLED LAB. BEGINNING TO THINK THAT WE DO NEED TO KEEP #CLOSEDBORDERS FOR #DOGSAFETY…

@PROTECTEASTOOLIANCALLCENTRE TO @JULIAFROMEASTOOLIA: WHAT DO YOU THINK ABOUT FACT IT'S NOT JUST DOGS THAT ARE GOING IF THE BORDER OPENS, IT'S OUR JOBS TOO? #CLOSEDBORDERS

NEW POST FROM @JULIAFROMEASTOOLIA: HEY EVERYONE. I CARE ABOUT EAST OOLIAN JOBS. THAT'S WHY - DELETE.

@JULIAFROMEASTOOLIA POSTS A PICTURE OF STRANGER. SHE SEEMS TO BE STARING AT JULIA LOVINGLY. IN FACT, THAT IS EXACTLY WHAT SHE'S DOING.

@JULIAFROMEASTOOLIA: BROKEN HEART.

SCENE NINE

In which Julia tries to guarantee her mother's job.

Friday morning.

The call centre. The boss's office.

JULIA sits across the desk from the CALL CENTRE BOSS in his office.

BOSS: Still or sparkling?

JULIA: Erm… nothing.

BOSS: Nothing?

JULIA: Tap.

BOSS: We don't have tap.

JULIA: Nothing then.

BOSS: Boiled sweet, candied fruit, gummy bear?

JULIA: No thanks.

BOSS: Right-wing newspaper, left-wing newspaper, centrist-liberal newspaper?

JULIA: No…

BOSS: I recommend the centrist-liberal paper.

JULIA: I don't read the paper.

BOSS: No one does. It's just supposed to make you feel like a valued customer.

JULIA: Okay but I still don't want it.
I want to know whether my mum's going to lose her job if the border opens?

BOSS: Who are you again?

JULIA: Tina's daughter.

BOSS: Who's Tina?

JULIA: She's worked for you for like ten years?

BOSS: All our employees are highly valued.

JULIA: So is that a no, she's not going to lose her job if the border opens?

BOSS: I can't confirm or deny that.

JULIA: But –

BOSS: I thought you were a social media star who's going to be an influencer for us?

JULIA: Erm, yeah, no – I just said that to get in. I don't really see how you can be an influencer for a call centre anyway.

Listen, you must know what you're going to do? If the border opens...

BOSS: We'll make the most sensible business decision at the time.

JULIA: What does that...?

BOSS: Our customers and our shareholders come first.

JULIA: What about your employees?

BOSS: All our employees are highly valued.

JULIA: If they're so highly valued then how come you didn't even know Mum's name?

Beat.

BOSS: If you're not going to have a boiled sweet, candied fruit, gummy bear, any kind of newspaper, bottled water or hot drink –

Did you want a hot drink? Coffee, tea, hot chocolate, herbal infusion, chai latte – I recommend caffeinated, they're highly addictive –

JULIA: No!

BOSS: In that case I think you should go.

Beat.

JULIA: I could post about you, you know. I have a lot of followers on InstaTwit. Including the mayor.

BOSS: Ah, the mayor. She's a very good friend of mine.

JULIA: …

BOSS: Thank you for coming. Your feedback is appreciated. Your call is important to us.

JULIA: But –

BOSS: Thank you for coming. Your feedback is appreciated. Your call is important to us.

SCENE TEN

In which Julia tries to condense her views about the border into one hundred and forty characters including spaces.

Friday afternoon.

The office of the East Oolian Reporter.

JULIA: I'm @JULIAFROMEASTOOLIA – I / mean, Julia.

JOURNALIST: @JULIAFROMEASTOOLIA!

JULIA: The mayor asked me to come – said you were doing an / article –

JOURNALIST: I know who you are! Thanks for coming. It's actually a listicle.

JULIA: A –

JOURNALIST: Yes, you're number five in our listicle of Five People Who Could Change History At The Town Hall This Sunday.

JULIA: Change history??

JOURNALIST: So listen, the angle we're looking for at the *East Oolian Reporter* is the dog thing.
You're fighting for closed borders because your poor rescue dog Fido –

JULIA: That's not her / name –

JOURNALIST: Sorry, Buster. The mayor briefed me / but –

JULIA: Stranger. Her name's Stranger.

JOURNALIST: Right…
Your poor dog – *dog* – he doesn't need a name –

JULIA: She's female.

JOURNALIST: Pardon?

JULIA: Stranger. She's female.

JOURNALIST: Don't you think it's weird when dogs are female?

JULIA: Like literally half of them are female.

JOURNALIST: Ha!
Okay, so… My dog – insert cute pic – was taken by illegal immigrants and that's why I'm fighting to keep the border closed, because I don't want anyone else to go through the same pain.

Something like that. Only in one hundred and forty characters including spaces. Do you have a pic of your dog cuddling a kitten?

JULIA: No. But I have a normal picture of her so people can see what she / looks like –

JOURNALIST: We can always sort it in post-production. Great. Thanks for coming.

JULIA: But I didn't say anything!

JOURNALIST: I thought you were happy with what I suggested?

JULIA: No! It's not what I think!

JOURNALIST: Oh! Okay.
So what *do* you think?

JULIA: …

JOURNALIST: Look, I'm going to be honest with you. A lot of people are wondering what the deal is with you. Why you went viral, why anybody should be listening to a 13-year-old anyway?

JULIA: …

JOURNALIST: I don't agree with them. But I do think you should be careful not to sound… muddled. So why don't you just let me deal with this? Okay?

JULIA: Forget it! I don't want to be in your stupid listicle, anyway.

JOURNALIST: What? Why?

You haven't spoken to Sarah from the *East Oolian Gazette* have you? Because I wouldn't trust her. She twists people's words.

JULIA: I haven't spoken to anyone. Just leave me alone!

Friday evening, 7pm.

@YOURMUM: I RAISED YOU AND NURTURED YOU AND NOW YOU'RE GOING TO BETRAY ME. LOVE, YOUR OWN MOTHER

@YOURDAD: I'M ON THE BRINK OF FINANCIAL RUIN AND IF YOU DON'T HELP I'M GOING TO FALL OFF THE EDGE. ALSO, WHERE ARE THE SPOONS???

@IHATEJULIAFROMEASTOOLIA: I AM NOT A BOT. I AM A PERSON WHO ACTUALLY REALLY HATES @JULIAFROMEASTOOLIA.

@YOURGRANDMA: GRANDPA ALMOST DIED IN THE WAR AND NOW THERE'S GOING TO BE ANOTHER ONE, THANKS TO YOU.

@VOICEINYOURHEAD: HA HA HA HA HA HA YOU HAVEN'T POSTED FOR AGES EVERYONE THINKS YOU SUCK AND GUESS WHAT? YOU SUCK! ALSO YOU LOOK FAT IN THOSE JEANS.

JULIA: Shut up!

NEW POST FROM @JULIAFROMEASTOOLIA: I CARE ABOUT DOGS. THAT'S ALL. NOT TRYING TO ANNOY ANYONE. I APOLI – APOLI –

JULIA: How do you spell that word???

DELETE.

@JULIAFROMEASTOOLIA: BUM FACE WHAT I DON'T KNOW. DELETE.

MEANWHILE, @FUNNYTINGE SEES @JULIAFROMEASTOOLIA'S LAST POST.

THE PHOTOGRAPH OF STRANGER, LOOKING
UP AT HER LOVINGLY. SOMEHOW THE IMAGE
REMINDS HIM OF HIS MOTHER, HIS BROTHER,
HIS FATHER.

@FUNNYTINGE: SAD FACE.

SCENE ELEVEN
In which Refugee Boy makes a life-changing decision.

Friday evening.

The SMUGGLER's house.

SMUGGLER opens the door to REFUGEE BOY.

SMUGGLER: What now?

REFUGEE BOY: Have you sold the dog yet?

SMUGGLER: Have you got me another dog yet?

REFUGEE BOY: …

> *SMUGGLER tries to close door in REFUGEE BOY's face.*

REFUGEE BOY: Wait!

I've got food.

SMUGGLER: …

REFUGEE BOY: If it gets too thin it won't sell for as much.

SMUGGLER: I'm not a monster! I am feeding it!

REFUGEE BOY: Okay but what am I going to do with this food? I might as well give it to the dog.

SMUGGLER: Is that fruit?

REFUGEE BOY: Don't dogs eat everything?

> *After a moment, SMUGGLER opens the door.*

SMUGGLER: This doesn't mean I'm going to sell it any quicker. It's all about the market. You got to get in at the top.

> *SMUGGLER lets REFUGEE BOY in.*

SMUGGLER: Dog's in here.

REFUGEE BOY is let into the basement.

REFUGEE BOY: Hey, dog.

STRANGER: Hey, human travelling boy.

> *(Aside, to audience.)* This is the one who stole me when he found me swimming across the boating lake back to my Julia-human and brought me to the smuggler-human.
>
> He's come to offer me grandma's fruit because he feels bad. He worries he's not a good person. Back home, his mother would look him in the eyes and say 'you're such a good boy'. And he believed it. But now he's not so sure.
>
> I'm a good dog and I've never had a moment's doubt about that.

REFUGEE BOY: I brought you some fruit….

STRANGER: *(Aside.)* How do I know all this? I know everything. I'm a dog.
No I would not like that fruit, travelling-human. It doesn't taste of anything.

REFUGEE BOY: What is it? Have you lost your appetite?

STRANGER: OF COURSE YOU IDIOT I'M PINING!

REFUGEE BOY: Shh! If you bark the smuggler will come down!

STRANGER: I'm stuck in a cage in a basement…

REFUGEE BOY: This cage is tiny…

STRANGER: I have to sleep in my own piss and shit.

REFUGEE BOY: You're covered in your own piss and shit…

STRANGER: There! You got it.

(Aside.) You see normally I go wherever Julia-human goes because wherever Julia-human goes smells like home. But this place smells only of me…

JULIA-HUMAN! JULIA-HUMAN! JULIA-HUMAN!

REFUGEE BOY: Shh! Be quiet!

SMUGGLER: What's going on down there?

STRANGER: I MISS MY JULIA-HUMAN!

REFUGEE BOY: I know! I know! You want to get out of here but you can't because…

SMUGGLER: I said what's going on there?

STRANGER: *(Aside.)* He's about to make a life-changing decision.

REFUGEE BOY unties STRANGER.

REFUGEE BOY: Let's go.

STRANGER: *(Aside.)* See?

Yes yes! Let's go let's go let's go!

REFUGEE BOY follows STRANGER out of the basement.

SMUGGLER: If you take that dog, your brother's done for!

REFUGEE BOY: No he's not because Julia's going to make them open the border and then we won't need you and your stupid pedalos!

REFUGEE BOY and STRANGER make a run for it.

SOCIAL MEDIA INTERLUDE 10

Saturday morning, 10am.

@FUNNYTINGE TO @JULIAFROMEASTOOLIA:
GOOD LUCK AT THE #TOWNHALL TOMORROW!
#OPENBORDERS #HOPEFUL #GRATEFUL

@JULIAFROMEASTOOLIA LOOKS AT THE POST
FROM @FUNNYTINGE.

SHE SCROLLS THROUGH HER OPTIONS….
THUMBS UP? NO. HAPPY FACE? SHE DOESN'T
FEEL HAPPY, SHE FEELS CONFUSED AND SAD…

SHE WRITES NOTHING.

SATURDAY MORNING, 11AM.

NEW POST FROM @JULIAFROMEASTOOLIA:
I DON'T WANT TO LET ANYONE DOWN BUT
I WON'T BE SPEAKING AT THE #TOWNHALL
ANYMORE. SORRY.

ONE – TWO – THREE – FOUR – TEN – FORTY-
FIVE ANGRY FACES. FORTY-SIX. SIXTY-THREE
ANGRY FACES.

@FUNNYTINGE: YOU DON'T WANT TO LET
ANYONE DOWN?

SCENE TWELVE

In which Julia tries to get Refugee Boy to eat a biscuit.

A few hours later.

JULIA's house.

REFUGEE BOY sits at the kitchen table with JULIA.

JULIA: Biscuit?

REFUGEE BOY: You said you were going to speak for open borders.

JULIA: People just want me to say whatever they want to hear. It's better not to say anything at all.

REFUGEE BOY: …

JULIA: Go on – have a biscuit –

REFUGEE BOY: You only want me to eat it to make you feel better! I'm tired of being grateful for nothing. A biscuit doesn't solve my problems.

JULIA: I didn't say it would.
Look, I know I let you down. You're a good person – you don't deserve this.

REFUGEE BOY: Nobody deserves it!

JULIA: Some people are here to take other people's jobs –

REFUGEE BOY: Because they're poor!
There's no war where I'm from. I lied.

Beat.

JULIA: So you are a migrant.

REFUGEE BOY: What's the difference? Running from poverty or running from bombs?

JULIA: War can kill you!

REFUGEE BOY: So can poverty!

JULIA: …

REFUGEE BOY: I don't think you're ever going to get your dog back.

JULIA: Why would you say that?

REFUGEE BOY: Because I don't think I'm ever going to get my brother back.

JULIA: What's your brother got to do with my dog?

REFUGEE BOY exits.

Saturday evening, 8pm.

@MAYOROFEASTOOLIA: SAD TO HEAR THAT @JULIAFROMEASTOOLIA IS TOO MENTALLY UNWELL TO SPEAK AT #TOWNHALL TOMORROW ON #CLOSEDBORDERS AND #DOGSOFEASTOOLIA. SENDING HER ALL THE BEST FOR A SPEEDY RECOVERY. DOG THEFT COSTS MINDS.

SCENE THIRTEEN

In which Refugee Boy tries to persuade Smuggler
to take Stranger back.

Early Sunday morning.

The SMUGGLER's house.

REFUGEE BOY knocks on SMUGGLER's door. He has STRANGER with him. SMUGGLER is wearing a bloody apron.

SMUGGLER: You've got some nerve.

REFUGEE BOY: I brought the dog back. The dog that escaped.

SMUGGLER: Escaped? I saw you take it out of here!

REFUGEE BOY: Only because it looked ill!
    It looks better now. It will sell for more money.

SMUGGLER: Don't be an idiot. I'd punch you in the face only
    I hate violence.

REFUGEE BOY: But I've brought it back!

SMUGGLER: Yeah and the bloody thing is snarling at me!

REFUGEE BOY: The market must have gone up by now.
    I can get you another one as well.

SMUGGLER: You missed your chance.
    Supply outstripped demand. The West Oolians have
    moved on. Dogs aren't hot anymore.

REFUGEE BOY: What?

SMUGGLER: The new must-have accessory is books.

REFUGEE BOY: Books? But –

SMUGGLER: Yeah I don't get it either.

But all the celebs are being pictured carrying books. So if you want your brother out then you'll have to get me cold hard cash.

REFUGEE BOY: I can't get a job. Everyone's checking papers.

SMUGGLER: Not everyone. Plenty of under the counter work. That's what you came here for, isn't it?

REFUGEE BOY: I'm clever. I'm good at drawing. I can spell words with three syllables. I can speak your language like a native. I came here to go to school and make something of myself.

SMUGGLER: La de da! What kind of jobs do you think I did before I turned my hand to this?

REFUGEE BOY: …

SMUGGLER: I even applied to be a border guard! Did a really good cover letter. Put in a semi-colon and everything. Didn't even get an interview.
We've all got to make money, mate. Most of us hate what we do. But we do it anyway, because we've got to survive. Get lost.

REFUGEE BOY: But what am I supposed to do with the dog?

SMUGGLER: Whatever you want. Get rid of it. Kill it. That's what I had to do with the rest.

SMUGGLER slams the door in REFUGEE BOY's face.

REFUGEE BOY looks down at STRANGER.

STRANGER: He's about to make a life-changing decision…

SCENE FOURTEEN

In which Julia tries to avoid the Town Hall debate.

JULIA's house.

Breakfast.

JULIA enters. GRANDMA, MOTHER and FATHER are sitting at the table. FATHER is greedily eating cereal. MOTHER sits in front of an empty bowl. GRANDMA is eating fruit.

GRANDMA: Finally! Young people are so sleepy.

JULIA: What's the point in getting up?

GRANDMA: Big day today.

JULIA: No it's not.

MOTHER: Now you're here, can you ask your father to pass the cereal please?

JULIA: Ask him yourself

FATHER: She doesn't need to ask…

FATHER pours the rest of cereal into his bowl and sends the empty box MOTHER's way.

GRANDMA: We're going to the Town Hall.

JULIA: I told you, I'm not speaking anymore.

MOTHER: Can I at least have some milk?

FATHER does the same thing with the milk.

MOTHER: What are you doing?

FATHER: Just thought you'd like to know how it feels to want a piece of the pie, and be told you can't have any.

MOTHER: Trust you to come up with a food analogy…

FATHER: Alright, then, to be hard-working, ready to
    contribute, and be told to go back home –

MOTHER: I'm not hard-working then?

JULIA: Guys!

MOTHER: I work twice as hard as you do!

JULIA: GUYS! Can you just do this at the debate?

   Beat.

FATHER: Actually, poppet, now you're not speaking…

JULIA: You're not going?

FATHER: Sunday's my admin day.

MOTHER: 'Admin'… Counting his pennies…

JULIA: Fine! You can go with Grandma then, Mum.

MOTHER: Sunday's my day off Julia, I've got to get the washing
    done, cook food for the week…

JULIA: What?

FATHER: I'll be at the vote though, don't you worry!

MOTHER: Me too – even if it kills me.

JULIA: So you guys are voting but not going to the debate?

MOTHER: …

FATHER: …

JULIA: I think that kind of says it all.

   JULIA stands and goes to GRANDMA.

JULIA: Come on, Grandma.

SCENE FIFTEEN
In which Julia takes a stand.

The Town Hall.

JULIA and GRANDMA enter the audience.

MAYOR is opening the Town Hall debate.

MAYOR: Welcome to the Town Hall debate.

When I ran for election I told you that I wanted to make East Oolia work for East Oolians. I told you that I'd close the border so we could take a moment to figure out how to deal with the swarms of people who pour across every day. Don't get me wrong: some of them are good people. But many of them are bad, bad people. People who aren't like us, who don't share our values or our way of life, people who should be sent back to where they –

The actor playing MAYOR stops.

ACTOR PLAYING MAYOR: Actually, can we stop for a minute?

I can't do this anymore.

This character sucks.

This moment sucks.

I'm supposed to stand up here and say this horrible stuff and then have a debate with… who? Julia and Grandma? Julia's too young to vote and Grandma – well, I don't want to be mean, but she's going to die soon.

Why aren't Mum and Dad here? Why didn't they come to the debate?

No, seriously. I'm asking you.

Because it's not just them, right? I mean, stuff is happening. Big stuff. Climate change. Brexit. Things that affect us - that affect you. And yeah, sure, some people do a lot, a lot of people do their best, but… Most of the time decisions are made and no one shows up.

I'm not going to lie. I'm the same. I say I'm going to go a protest but then the day rolls round and I don't. I sign the petition but then I don't bother persuading other people to sign. Sometimes I don't even vote, even though I can.

What's stopping me?

What's stopping you?

I mean, who thinks politics is boring?

Show of hands.

Who thinks it's confusing?

Show of hands.

And who thinks politics is important?

Show of hands.

So what do you care about? Are you fighting for it?

The audience responds.

The STAGE MANAGER enters and cuts them off.

STAGE MANAGER: What the fridge?

ACTOR PLAYING MAYOR: Sorry, I just… you know I hate this bit.

STAGE MANAGER: Okay but The Writer's in.

ACTOR PLAYING MAYOR: Really? But she never comes.

STAGE MANAGER: Well, she's here. And she says you need to trust the script. That she put a lot of thought into it, especially the ending. She's crying.

ACTOR PLAYING MAYOR: Crying?

STAGE MANAGER: She definitely had tears in her eyes.

ACTOR PLAYING MAYOR: Okay, fine.

STAGE MANAGER exits.

I'll catch you guys up. I give a really long speech and then a few of you tell me what you think about the border – and whatever you say, I say –

ACTOR PLAYING MAYOR transitions back to MAYOR.

MAYOR: Let me be clear – you've all been very clear.

We're going to take back control.

East Ooli-exit means East Ooli-exit.

Now, let's vote!

REFUGEE BOY enters, with STRANGER. He takes the mic.

REFUGEE BOY: Wait! Before you vote! Where's Julia? I've got something for her…

JULIA stands.

JULIA: Stranger!

STRANGER runs into JULIA's arms.

It is a joyful reunion.

JULIA: You found her!

REFUGEE BOY: Everybody deserves to be with their family.

JULIA: Thank you!

MAYOR: Right… As I was saying, let's vote –

JULIA: I want to speak!

MAYOR: Julia…

We were sorry not to hear from you earlier – and sorry
about your mental health / issues –

JULIA: I know what I think now.

MAYOR: You've got your dog, so I don't really see any need –

JULIA: But I think you're wrong – I / think –

MAYOR: I'm afraid you missed your opportunity –

GRANDMA: Let her speak!

JULIA: ...

MAYOR: Okay, we need to get on now –

JULIA: You say migrants are bad people who steal dogs, but I
think migrants are good people.
I know that now. Because the thing about strangers, is that
they turn into friends. You just have to give them a chance.
I don't have a vote. But if I did, I know how I'd vote.
I'd vote to open the border.

GRANDMA stands and starts clapping.

MAYOR: That's all very sweet, but who do you think stole
your dog in the first place? Who stole my dogs? Who stole
the thousands of East Oolian dogs that have been taken?

JULIA: ...

MAYOR: People are living in fear. You can come up with
fluffy little slogans, but it doesn't change the fact that what
people want most of all right now, is security.

And that's what I offer by keeping the border closed.

Now, let's vote.

Sunday evening, 6pm.

@MAYOROFEASTOOLIA: THANKS TO ALL OUR SPEAKERS AND THANKS TO THE AUDIENCE AT THE #TOWNHALL! GREAT DEBATE!

THE VOTES ARE IN… RESULTS SOON. #DEMOCRACYINACTION

@JULIAFROMEASTOOLIA: PRAYING MONKEY EMOJI

@FUNNYTINGE: PRAYING MONKEY EMOJI

SPONSORED AD: @SECURITYSOLUTIONS: SHARE PRICES UP 230%! INVEST NOW!

…………..

@MAYOROFEASTOOLIA: THE PEOPLE OF EAST OOLIA HAVE SPOKEN.

THE BORDER WITH WEST OOLIA WILL… REMAIN CLOSED.

#CLOSEDBORDERS

SCENE SIXTEEN

In which Julia tries to bring everyone together over stew.

That evening.

JULIA's house.

Dinner.

REFUGEE BOY, GRANDMA, MOTHER and JULIA sit around the table. STRANGER is on JULIA's lap.

There is a pot of stew on the table.

MOTHER is eating.

JULIA: Where's Dad?

MOTHER: Upstairs with a headache.

GRANDMA: He was called a 'dirty westie' on his way home and told to go back to where he came from.

JULIA: What? Dad was abused in the street for being West Oolian?

MOTHER: It's ridiculous. He's only half...

JULIA: That doesn't make it better!
Imagine if you were told this isn't your home?

MOTHER: Well, I –

JULIA: Yeah. You wouldn't be, would you? Because you're East Oolian.

Beat.

MOTHER: Why is no one eating?

REFUGEE BOY: Thank you, it looks delicious...

MOTHER: Eat it then!

JULIA's phone gets an alert.

MOTHER: Julia…

JULIA checks it.

@IHEARTDOGS TO @JULIAFROMEASTOOLIA: DOESN'T YOUR MUM WORK AT THE CALL CENTRE? IT'S MOVING TO WEST OOLIA.

JULIA: Wow. Okay.

The call centre's moving to West Oolia.

MOTHER: What?

JULIA checks her phone.

JULIA: @EASTOOLIANCALLCENTRE: WE ARE SORRY TO SAY THAT WE ARE ANNOUNCING WITH IMMEDIATE EFFECT OUR RELOCATION TO WEST OOLIA. THE BUSINESS CASE IS CLEAR AND WE HAVE TO PUT OUR CUSTOMERS AND SHAREHOLDERS FIRST.

MOTHER: But – I don't understand –

GRANDMA: I suppose even if people can't, businesses can go where they want. Dear.

MOTHER: This is a joke.

MOTHER pushes away her plate.

GRANDMA: Do you know why the fruit tastes of nothing?

JULIA: …

GRANDMA: Because it's all mass produced, that's why. It wasn't always like that. Once upon a time an apple tasted of apple, and a pear of pear. But of course, they weren't all good, you see? Some of them had worms. Now, you people work nonsense jobs for nonsense pay and in your

lunchbreaks you eat a sort-of-pear that tastes of nothing
but at least it's exactly the same as the last one you ate and
of course there are no worms… And that gives you the
only sense of control you have in a life that otherwise feels
like you're in freefall.

So when the mayor comes along and says, I know you
feel out of control, I know you feel desperate, well don't
worry, I've got the answer! Throw out the foreigners! You
fall for it. My own daughter-in-law fell for it. But that's just
pure worm that is, there's no fruit in that at all. Instead
of throwing out the foreigners who are taking away your
nonsense jobs, you should throw away the nonsense jobs!
You should throw away the whole nonsense system!

That's who the real enemy is.

So yes, the joke's on you.

GRANDMA stands.

MOTHER: I know exactly who the enemy is.

> *(To REFUGEE BOY.)* It's you. I bet you'd work the same job
> as me for half the pay.

REFUGEE BOY: Right now, I'd work anywhere for anything.

MOTHER: Told you!

JULIA: But he shouldn't!

> That's what Grandma's saying with all that weird fruit stuff….
> Nobody should. You hate your job. It doesn't *mean* anything
> – you're trying to sell things to people who don't want them.

> He's a good person. He's like you – just trying to feed
> himself and his family.

REFUGEE BOY: I'm not a good person. You need to stop
saying that. I'm not a good person.

JULIA: Yes you are. You found Stranger –

REFUGEE BOY: But the mayor was right – I was the one who stole her!

JULIA's phone goes.

@HUGABEAR SHARES A CLIP OF @JULIAFROMEASTOOLIA SAYING 'MIGRANTS ARE GOOD PEOPLE' DURING HER SPEECH AT THE TOWN HALL WITH A LOVE HEART.

JULIA: *(To REFUGEE BOY.)* I don't understand…

REFUGEE BOY: I was scared.

JULIA: You know what it's like to be separated from someone you love.

REFUGEE BOY: Exactly. And I was scared of losing him. I still am.

REFUGEE BOY stands.

REFUGEE BOY: I'll go.

MOTHER pushes away her plate.

MOTHER: I'm not hungry either –

JULIA: Sit down!
Everyone just sit down.

MOTHER: Why? You want to look at your phone, Grandma thinks I'm a joke, and this boy – who's clearly a liar and a thief – wants to –

JULIA: Because we all eat together in this family!

Grandma?

GRANDMA sits down.

GRANDMA: I'm sorry, Tina.

I should have spoken to you with more respect.

MOTHER sits down.

JULIA: And you!

REFUGEE BOY: Me?

JULIA: I'm scared, too. Right now I'm scared of you.

Because I don't understand – I really don't understand – how you could do that.

REFUGEE BOY: You don't know what it's like to be me –

JULIA: You don't know what it's like to be me!

Look, we're all scared. Everyone in this family is, anyway. No one listens to anyone and everyone's angry and honestly I think we're scared of each other. I don't even know how that happened.

So I'll do you a deal. I promise to listen to you if you promise to be honest with me. Because maybe there aren't good people and bad people. Maybe there are just people.

REFUGEE BOY: If you'll do the same for me.

JULIA: I will.

REFUGEE BOY sits down.

JULIA's phone goes. She ignores it.

JULIA: And we're all going to eat this stew.

Alright Mum?

Beat.

MOTHER: I'll go get your father.

Sunday evening, 10pm.

@JULIAFROMEASTOOLIA POSTS A PICTURE OF HER BELOVED COCKAPOO STRANGER SITTING IN HER LAP. SHE APPEARS TO BE PERFECTLY CONTENTED. IN FACT, SHE IS PERFECTLY CONTENTED.

@JULIAFROMEASTOOLIA COMMENTS: HOME AT LAST.

SONG OF HOME

What is home?
A patch of grass that you've pissed on?
The person that you're sitting on?
The smell or taste
Of your favourite human?
Is it the song of a bird?
The hug of a neighbour?
The shade of your passport?
Or the feeling you get when you're safe?

They say that home is where the heart is
But the heart is prone to wander
I'll take my home where I find it
I'll make my home where I land
What choice do I have?

What is home?
The mother that you've drunk from?
The river that you've swum across?
The dreamless sleep
That comes from being at rest?
Is it the taste of a dish?
The sound of a language?
The view from the window?
Or the feeling you get when you're safe?

They say that home is where the heart is
But the heart is prone to wander
I'll take my home where I find it
I'll make my home where I land
What choice do I have?

By the same author

Octopus
9781786821935

WWW.OBERONBOOKS.COM

Follow us on Twitter @oberonbooks
& Facebook @OberonBooksLondon

www.ingramcontent.com/pod-product-compliance
Ingram Content Group UK Ltd.
Pitfield, Milton Keynes, MK11 3LW, UK
UKHW022130020325
455697UK00009B/115